From Fear and Failure — To The Finish Line:

Unleash Your Potential,
and Discover the Champion Within

To Connie

Keep dreaming!

Cindy

By

Cindy Buckner Starke, MD, PhD

Wife, Mother, Doctor, Full Iron-Distance Triathlete

ISBN-10:1530642760

ISBN-13: 978-1530642762

For orders, or information, contact Cindy at http://cindystarke. com/contact

I dedicate this book to my family: Steve, Jessica, and Wyatt—you make crossing the finish lines of my life so sweet.

You give my life meaning, and I love you dearly.

Contents

Acknowledgments

I would like to thank God for putting this dream in my heart. I thank Him for my tenacity, my determination, my grit, my brain, my gifts and talents, and the ability to endure the most difficult race in the world. I can't wait to see what benefits come from the story that follows in these tear-stained pages.

I thank God for giving me my husband, Steve, for being the first person to make me aware of what all I am capable of. Thank you, Steve, for being so devoted to us, for being such a hard worker and great example to our kids. Thank you for your endless caring for the kids on all the days and nights I was gone with training and now writing the book to share my story.

I thank my kids, for making me analyze my priorities daily. You've taught me so much more about life than I believe I will ever teach you.

Huge hugs to Wyatt, for all the times you would go to the pool with me during my long training swims just to keep me company and for biking alongside me while I ran. I could always count on you to ask me how my training went as soon as I walked in the door. Having you there to witness me cross the finish line at Beach to Battleship, and actually cross it with me, elated me in ways I could never describe. You always challenge me to eat healthier and be the best version of me possible. You are a champion and a leader to all who know you.

Jessica, you supplied me with endless playlists on my phone and constant laughter. You are the best partner for all the breaks I needed, whether that be Starbucks runs, Brusters, or Nashville for the Taylor Swift "1989" tour concert. I loved watching you create your own YouTube channel showcasing your amazing God-given talents of singing and performing. I hope that my daring to get in the arena and strive for Ironman will always show you how you can accomplish absolutely anything you set your mind to!

I also want to thank the following—

My mom, whose constant presence, unconditional love, and incessant support has guided me to be a wonderful, caring person. Your presence at all three triathlons meant the world to me. At each event, you fed me and cleaned me up, literally and figuratively. Thanks to my dad, who taught me about hard work, being honest, and always being a supporter in my life. I appreciate more than ever your running background and your ability to understand just how well I was doing as I went along. Thanks to my brother and sister, my lifelong companions. David is my free-spirited soul mate, and Gina my God-centered compass in life. We are so very blessed to be so close.

My training partner, Lisa Morris. Though the finish lines we crossed were almost 550 miles and eight weeks apart, we finished! We did it, girl! I've never seen anyone so dedicated to their goal. Thank you for being so dedicated to me through it all. I am glad I had you and that we went through it all together. I could have never done my second full Iron-distance triathlon without you there.

My mindset coach, Andy Lowe, for instilling in me the mere thought of Ironman. For listening and correcting and guiding and shifting my mindset, week after week, for two straight years. You showed me how to accomplish the impossible dream, and walked me, painfully at times, through challenging the deeply ingrained fears I'd held onto for dear life for decades. You took me from a chicken to a peacock! My life is forever changed.

My friend Melanie Churchwell, for lovingly putting her foot in my rear to teach me to start believing in myself and for training me to become a group fitness instructor way back in the day. You started it all, girl. You ran right next to me, talking me through every painful step of my first 5K race after a ten year hiatus, and stayed while I won third in my age group. You constantly make me dream bigger and know better.

My nutrition coach, Betsy Pake, for teaching me how to fuel my body to slay the event and being there for me as a constant encouragement. Thank you also for showing me how easy it was to become an author.

My Ironman friends—Ginny Crumley, for being my idol in the sport and displaying such humility and persistence. Mitch Salain, for all the encouragement you gave me on those dark mornings at Frances Meadows and for letting me pick your brain on how to train. Bryan Baumgardner, for the constant "what if?" questions and teaching me it was absolutely acceptable to do most of my training on the trainer. Thank you Denise Novicki, for joining me on the half, and running back and getting me. Randy and Susan Allen, for answering all my questions about the sport. And Drew Abernathy, for showing me how to just open up my dang mouth and breathe!

My swimming coach, Andy Deichert. No one but you could make me feel like such a rockstar at 5:30 am! You showed me how to believe in myself as a swimmer, and showed me a 44-year-old CAN learn new tricks! I still can't really believe I went from not being able to swim twenty seconds without gasping for air and having my heart rate in the 170s to being able to swim a solid 2.4 miles calmly and collectedly. That's all because of you. Your boisterous, loud, upbeat personality made it easy for me to do my part - just show up!

My open-water swim coach, Joy Kelleher. I never knew I could sweat in the freezing water until I did your workouts. You selflessly gave your time and resources just to make me better. Your message on Facebook that day I got my DNF was the most palpable example of God sending me the exact angel I needed to muscle through my failure and turn the whole saga into a success. Thank you.

A special heartfelt thanks goes to all my dearest friends who have shared in my life's journey: Nicole Dullaghan, Laura Corley, Dolly Sinha, Milene Argo, Monica Green, Nicole Anderson, Halla Shami, Jeba Pandian, Alene Arenas, Stacey Terry, Karen Towles, Amy Phillips, Juliana Roca-Martinez, Carolina Lombardi, and Wanda Adams. Each of your existences has woven a rich, unique color of thread into the fabric of my life.

I have had a slew of mentors along the way, too, who acted as guides as I carved my special path in life. You all validated me, encouraged me to become the best student, worker, and doctor possible, and I'm indebted to each of you, for now and for always: Grant Bennett, Marci Wendelken, Claude Pickelsimer, Miriam Parker, and Tom DiFulco.

My band of marine brothers—Sean Dullaghan, Keith Bowen, and Bryan Baumgardner—for teaching me what a "hard charger" is and for teaching me so much about the military during my Ironman journey!

Thanks to Chandler Bolt and everybody in the Self-Publishing School community. I would have never become an author without your organized guidance.

My accountabilibuddy, author Jamie White Wyatt, for being there for me and for praying for me when my writing was difficult. When you pray, it goes directly to the source! Your prayer for stamina, words, and more stamina led to my miraculous ability to sit for sixteen straight hours and edit my book front to back, increasing my word count from ten thousand to seventeen thousand . . . in one day!

My book-writing coach, Emily Rose, for being so straightforward with me. I was her star student and brought her to tears just summarizing my story to her.

My book editor, Nancy Pile, whose Harvard education and endurance biker background was the perfect match for me. Thanks for being tough on me and telling me exactly what I needed to do to make my book convey exactly what I was after.

My book cover designer Ida Fia Sveningsson. She knew exactly what I wanted and a million times more even though I was unable to verbalize it.

The administrators at Longstreet Clinic—Mimi Collins, Cindy Stazsak, Jullie King, and Margaret Spratlin—for showcasing my journey in so many ways to support me, including placing me in the spotlight at the Women Go Red event. That meant the world to me. Thank you.

Introduction

Failure.

Just the thought of failure is terrifying. It keeps us up at night. Failure is something we want to avoid at all costs. The thought of failing at something makes most of us not even attempt to do something new. We sometimes stay in unfulfilling jobs because of our fear of the unknown. We live small, comfortable lives inside our small, comfortable comfort zones not because we love it, but just to keep failure at bay.

If we fail at something big, like a marriage or a business venture, we get stopped dead in our tracks. We make vows never to date again, never to make ourselves vulnerable again. We try to force ourselves to enjoy being alone, to never try to love again. We try to fit our "round selves" back into "square boxes" because it seems safer or at least, easier—even though the fit isn't quite right . . .

But failure is inevitable, really. Through failure we learn to improve ourselves. We learn to grow. We learn to get it right or at least, get it better. We simply cannot let moments, or even weeks, of embarrassment shame us into not trying again. We cannot allow fleeting disappointment to shackle us into an existence of the status quo.

I recently endured twenty-one hours a week of training, six days a week, for two solid years, preparing for half Iron-distance and Ironman competitions. I spent thousands of dollars on registration fees, travel costs, and gear. Finally, I competed in my first Ironman, but I FAILED TO FINISH MY RACE!

I suffered the devastating letdown of receiving a DNF—*did not finish*—a disqualification because I was ten minutes short of a cutoff time for biking. So while I didn't decide to stop and drop out of the race, I was disqualified because my performance wasn't good enough. I tried my hardest—and it wasn't good enough—so I was disqualified. That's how I failed.

Failing to complete that race hurt, a lot. My failure left me embarrassed and humiliated—in front of everyone at the competition and then in front of everyone back home, friends, family, and acquaintances—from work, my children's school, church, my neighborhood, the pool, the bike shop, the lake, etc. I had to share the failure repeatedly with all the people who asked how my race went—

Q: Cindy, did you have that race yet? How was it?

A: Yeah. It was last weekend. Well, my time wasn't good enough, so I was disqualified in the bike portion.

Q: But weren't you practicing for years for it? So how could your time not be good enough? What happened?

Some people would jump to wrong conclusions—

Q: Oh, the swim took you too long, so you ran out of time?

A: No. I actually finished the swim within the allotted time given.

Q: Didn't your coach tell you about the cutoffs?

A: I was told, but I didn't commit the specific times to memory. It was my job to know. But I was overwhelmed with all the details. He can't spoon-feed me everything.

Q: What? Time cutoffs? You paid so much money! They should let you finish anyway!

A: But the race is governed by necessarily strict rules to protect the safety of the athletes.

It was awful. It was exhausting trying to explain the story to a dozen new, curious minds each week. I felt like giving up on ever dreaming again. Dreaming big means you could fail big. Then you have to rehash and dissect the anatomy of the failure repeatedly. I began to think maybe it would be better to just not dream such big dreams. Go back to being small. When no one expects anything big, you don't have to explain yourself, and you just exist in comfortable, easy mediocrity.

Up to now, I had been able to complete everything I set my mind to. And not just complete, but do it with honors! This big failure stuff basically was unchartered territory for me, and I hated what it felt like. I felt so exposed and judged. I was embarrassed, humiliated, and ashamed of myself.

Profound, debilitating depression followed. In its aftermath, I never again wanted to share my aspirations with anyone. I wanted to hide in a hole and pretend that I never tried something new. I wanted to avoid public embarrassment. I wanted to avoid everybody.

My failure was an epic letdown! I was heartbroken and mad. It seemed the prior two years of grueling training were an absolute waste of time. I vowed never to be that vulnerable again.

Choosing Freedom over Fear-dom

Left unchecked, feelings of failure can paralyze you. They confine you to smaller and smaller areas. You're afraid to venture out of your comfort zone because you fear getting hurt again or fear messing up again. You begin arranging your life around safer circumstances and lower expectations. You put yourself in a cage, lock the door, and hide the key. It's a suffocating way to not really live. I know because I've been there. But I also managed to break through the bars of that cage I'd created for myself—and that's what I want to show you how to do too!

From Fear and Failure—To the Finish Line can help you move past your fears of failure. It is for people who are tired of living uneventful lives characterized by being in a rut and feeling like just another nameless face in the rat race of life. This book is for people who are tired of watching from the sidelines while others accomplish great things.

LEARN HOW YOU CAN:

—Go for promotions and get them.

—Join a class, group, or organization that you are interested in but have been hesitant about.

—Sign up for triathlons and cross the finish line.

—Surround yourself by those who are daring to be bold with their lives.

—Accomplish your goals and dreams.

—Get out of your comfort zone and change your daily routine

—Dare to be different from your regular self and then do it! Be your best self!

From Fear and Failure—To the Finish Line is for anyone who is tired of settling for mediocrity. You simply need to believe that a life of epic awesomeness is within your reach!

As a wife, mother, friend, endurance triathlete, and doctor, I've had my fair share of failures. I failed my driver's license test the first time I took it. I have failed examinations. I have had to pronounce patients dead whom I thought I could save. I have failed at being honest at times with my husband. I have failed to give God credit for talents I claim to be the prideful owner of.

I have failed sorely at keeping friendships I thought would last a lifetime. I have said things to my children I would give anything to take back. I've burned dinners and ruined cakes that I had invested a great deal of money and time into. I've not gotten jobs that surely would have been perfect for me. My dream house has been lost before to someone else's contract. My failures may have set me back, but they did not define me or stop me from trying again.

When I applied for a MD–PhD medical scientist training program, I was rejected. Instead of rethinking my future, I did just the opposite—I promptly asked the admissions director to reopen my file to interview me again. I was not only granted admission into the training program, but I also received a full scholarship, including a yearly stipend, for all seven years. My refusal to accept failure and my subsequent willingness to have twenty seconds of boldness and courage landed me a 210 thousand dollar full-ride scholarship. I was able to start my life as a doctor completely debt-free, all because I refused to let failure define me.

But don't think that cleared me from ever grappling with failure again. It has happened again and again in my life. There have been times when I thought failure—or even the possibility of it—would conquer me (the triathlon fail, for example), but it didn't. I didn't let it. It wasn't easy, but I developed a system to stay strong, curious, and up for another try, even when I failed in a previous attempt.

The Cindy Starke Success System

Anyone who struggles with failure can experience monumental, life-changing breakthroughs by implementing the tips, mindset shifts, and universal truths presented in this book. A number of students, athletes, and doctors whom I know have already begun to experience success from following the lessons I share in *From Fear and Failure—To the Finish Line*.

One example is Daniel Cobb, a full-time neurologist and married father of two, who unfortunately suffers from devastating psoriatic and rheumatoid arthritis. After implementing my system, Daniel is challenging the limitations that his family and other doctors have placed on him his entire life. As a thirty-six-year-old with a lifetime of crippling stiffness and two surgeries, he is seriously considering signing up for an Ironman in 2017. Though for years now he has been mountain biking and swimming twice daily just to maintain his flexibility, my journey has now inspired him to start running again. And you know what happens when you add running to a base of biking and swimming? That's right—a triathlon.

If you incorporate into your life the principles clearly delineated in my book, I promise you will never let failure define you again. I promise you'll begin to realize your potential, dare to dream big, and embark on the adventure that life is meant to be.

Don't be someone who misses out on opportunities and never realizes their goals. Dream big. Live a life you're proud of—a life with no regrets.

The methods presented in *From Fear and Failure—To the Finish Line* can help anyone move past failure. All you need to do to live the life of your dreams is keep reading. Each chapter presents new insights into moving past failure. Once you have broken through your own barriers, fears, and self-limiting thoughts, you will become more successful and inspire others. Are you ready to get started?

1

Fear's Roots

From Childhood to Adulthood

From birth, fear and I seemed to have become best friends. Fear became a mainstay in my life, a constant presence. Due to several unfortunate events in my childhood, fear for my safety and fear of my health potentially failing at any moment became my norm.

I was born with a rash. My parents didn't want to take me out in public until I was at least six weeks old. Incessant sneezing attacks led to a diagnosis of severe allergic rhinitis. Two decades of four injections a week left my arms in tender, reddened knots. I had other close calls that heightened my fear too. I almost drowned in a partially frozen lake when I was in elementary school. The next year I almost lost an eye because I reached down to pet the wrong dog one sunny Sunday afternoon, and he bit me.

An ear polyp removal at age fifteen and subsequent reconstructive surgery left me partially deaf in one ear. At age sixteen, I was in a devastating car accident and broke my jawbone. My mouth was wired shut for weeks. I wasted down to a measly ninety pounds. Undiagnosed scoliosis gave me a funky posture and chronic pain, which, to this day, require constant preventive maintenance.

Another car accident occurred when my children were toddlers. I totaled my car and was afraid to drive on the highway for months. All of these events were seared in my memory. To put it mildly, I had an overly developed sense of caution. Dangers, enemies, and disaster lurked everywhere.

The most recent accident occurred at age forty. I was trying to learn the art of clipping into bike pedals—you know, those shoes that lock into the bicycle pedal. In one instance in my learning, I fell off my bike less than a hundred feet from my house, onto my outstretched hand. I was cautiously biking slowly, not realizing that building up momentum on the bike was the way to stay upright, moving, and safe. I biked so slowly that I ended up toppling over and severely damaging that outstretched hand.

I had a seventeen thousand dollar reconstructive surgical procedure on my thumb, followed by several months of occupational therapy and a cast. I was unable to tie my children's shoes for months because of a bulky cast that went halfway up my arm. A result: fear of biking overtook me. I decided to never get on a bike again.

The other result was even more devastating because fear didn't just overtake me. It seemed to trickle into the hearts and minds of my children. It quickly became my family's mantra, "Mom will never clip into a bike again. Clipping into a bike is dangerous. Don't try new things. New things are dangerous. You could get killed. Did you hear of so-and-so that got killed on a bike? Yep! He was clipped in, and a motorist ran over his head."

In summary, I developed a lifetime of crippling, limiting thoughts. That mindset prevented me forever from living the life of my dreams. These beliefs were engraved deep in my psyche and seemed to be invading the psyches of my children too.

Read on to see how I quickly challenged every one of those limiting thoughts I grew up with, both in my family and in myself. I realized a bigger, brighter, bolder version of me was yet to come.

2

From Letdown to Not Letting Up

Spotlight—Off Me & On Them

I decided after the bike accident that it was safer to pour into my children instead of developing any new skills of my own. So I spent my days watching my kids and their teams practice and compete in several sports.

I started becoming aware of what my husband and I were preaching to our children too. Our eleven-year-old son Wyatt has a dream of playing baseball for the University of Georgia Bulldogs. Our daughter Jessica has a fierce natural talent in music and is profoundly inspired by Taylor Swift's bold style of songwriting and performing.

We always told Wyatt that he could make that baseball team if he does one thing: outwork everybody else. Success has little to do with talent or luck. It's just pure hard work. So day after day, season after season, I watch my son develop the skills that we teach him. He works on the tee, he catches pop-up flies, he pitches and pitches and then pitches some more.

Jessica advanced to the A-team in her middle school volleyball team and played on the starting lineup in tennis after weeks of trying hard. She faced some incredible fears and stage fright, and started performing her music live on stage exactly a year after getting her first guitar lesson. What a go-getter!

The Big American Letdown

Ever notice how we tell our kids they can do anything, cheering them on to big victories each season? This could be spelling bees, sports, robotics competitions, and plays. The common American mistake is that in the meantime, we adults do nothing for ourselves. The status quo, the daily grind, work and pay bills— that's enough for us.

How can we pour into our kids' dreams and not dream ourselves? How could I not practice what I was preaching? How could I keep asking them to do something, to set a big goal and chip away daily at it, if I was unwilling to do it myself?

My 180

Once I realized that I was essentially preaching one thing to my kids and practicing the opposite myself, I wanted to learn just what I was capable of. However, I had somehow lost my ability to dream. So what did I do? I hired the Atlanta-based businessman and mindset coach Andy Lowe, founder of Renegade

Concepts, to teach me how to break through barriers of what I believed was possible in my life.

ONE—Andy first advised me that the only way to teach myself to dream big and pursue a big dream was to literally put it into practice. He advised that I choose some goal that seemed impossible. The examples he suggested were to build a house, hike the Appalachian Trail, or complete an endurance fitness competition. It had to be something that took two years of daily, consistent effort to prepare for.

In response, I chose a full Ironman Triathlon: 140.6 miles total—2.4 miles swimming, followed by 112 miles bicycling, followed by 26.2 miles running, all done consecutively without stopping between each stage.

TWO—the next step from there was to break down this monumental, monstrously huge competition into manageable pieces. It's not about closing your eyes and just jumping into the big impossible. It's about taking the impossible by the horns and dividing it into manageable pieces that you work with daily.

We divided the Ironman Triathlon into two big steps. First, I would spend seven months training for a half Iron-distance triathlon. This distance was a total of 70.3 miles: 1.2 miles of swimming, then a 56-mile bike ride, and then a 13.1-mile run. Second, after I competed in the half, I would spend eight months training for the full Ironman.

Walk Your Talk

You too can practice what we teach our children—to set big goals and practice each day to achieve them. You too can break out of the rut of your daily routine and make a 180-degree turn in your life. In the next chapter, I walk you through this—how to take that huge dream, the one that scares you to death, and break it down into daily practices.

3

Devise a Plan & Commit

Once I realized that dreaming shouldn't stop once we exit childhood, I established my big dream—the grueling Ironman Triathlon. So that you can understand how to take your big dream and make it into a reality by breaking it down into manageable pieces, I'll share how I divided my triathlon training into daily practices.

I am going to share with you my plan for preparing for the half Iron-distance triathlon (remember—it was my first hurdle. The full Ironman came next!). No, I'm not sharing this with you because I want your big dream to be to compete in an Ironman competition. I'm sharing my training plan, so you can use it as a model in creating your own plan for success.

When you read over my plan, I want you to notice and take away with you these crucial elements:

- How very small and incremental the steps are in my plan

- How my own comfort level and feeling of safety are never ignored and only slowly, slowly challenged
- How my plan takes into account both my physical and psychological needs
- How my success at mastering very small steps gives me confidence and the positive reinforcement to expand my comfort zone
- How I don't do it alone. I have coaches, training partners, friends, and even my children with me when I can.

So please notice how all these crucial elements play out in my plan to achieve my BIG DREAM because when you make your plan, you'll want these elements guiding you too.

The Breakdown

Time—I started in April to prepare for an October half Iron-distance triathlon. This was the first step to be able to complete the full Ironman race in November of the following year. Notice how I gave myself plenty of time to become fully prepared physically and mentally to achieve both the half Iron-distance triathlon and my big goal, the full Ironman.

Cycling, the Psychological and Physical Sides— Learning to bike and being patient through the process was the most difficult mental achievement of this journey. I quickly learned I had to let go of the past. Injuries of the past didn't have to continue to hinder me from growing. Andy was pivotal in walking me through this psychological journey. I'd been subconsciously holding myself back for fear of repeating the past.

Something very important that I learned was to determine my own comfort zone and work within it. Typically, this meant taking very small steps that perhaps others would find too small, but for me were just right. For example, to overcome my fear of biking with clipless pedals (the kind where the shoe locks into the pedal. Remember I had that major accident biking with this type of pedal?) and master it, I biked for weeks wearing one tennis shoe and one clipped-in biking cleat. I didn't care if I didn't look "cool" or whatever—I cared about learning a new skill in a way that met my needs.

Another example: I noticed if I biked with friends, I unwisely would bike on routes they were comfortable with, but that I was highly uncomfortable with. We'd bike on streets with too much traffic or on routes with too many hills to maneuver for my skillset. Instead, I increased my confidence by biking circuits in parking lots. I got comfortable being able to simply remove one foot from the pedal and then repeated the skill using two cleats. Talk about small, incremental steps!

Once I was ready, I ventured out on bike rides with friends. I tried joining a biking group, but it was difficult to feel like I was not slowing the other members down. So again, I didn't force myself to do something I was very uncomfortable with. Instead, I found other routes and groups that met my comfort, safety, and fitness needs.

My favorite place to bike was the Silver Comet, a multipurpose trail. I loved having only pedestrians, cyclists, and the occasional roller blader to navigate around. I felt safe, comfortable, and confident on this trail, which is how I needed to feel to overcome both my physical and psychological hurdles around biking.

I had to be very diligent and strategic with my biking and how it interfaced with my work schedule. I work as a hospitalist, with a seven-days-on, seven-days-off schedule. When I'm on, I'm on pager call for twenty-four hours a day. I have to be no farther than thirty minutes from the hospital, so I can quickly tend to a patient's potential needs, in person if needed.

On my working weeks, I could not travel to the Silver Comet Trail to cycle, as it is located too far away from the hospital. Therefore, on workweeks, after patient rounds, I'd drive to the nearby Cool Springs Road and simply bike up and down the road, traversing five miles away from my car and then five miles back, repeatedly to get in the mileage. This kept me close enough to my car should a nurse need me at the hospital.

Eventually, doing this Cool Springs Road riding became too stressful, so I borrowed a trainer from my biker friend, Melanie Churchwell, attached my bike to it, and completed all bike rides in my living room. It was boring biking for hours in my living room, but I didn't need the added stress of patient or nurse complaints that I couldn't be at the hospital in a timely fashion. So again, to get in the training I needed, I didn't force myself to do something that stressed me out. I worked with the reality of my life and didn't fight it.

In contrast, on my off weeks, I would get up at 4:30 am and arrive at the Comet at 7 am to do my long-distance cycling. My husband would take the kids to school if it was needed, or in the summer, I would be able to complete the ride and arrive back home to be with my kids before noon.

Swimming, at the Pool and Lake—I met a local swimming coach, Andy Deichert, through a master's swimming course at the local aquatic center. He taught me how to swim freestyle in a pool.

I met with Coach Deichert at least two times a week at 5:30 am until I perfected the skills necessary to complete the long swim. I can't express how crucial it was for me to know that if I would do my part and just get there in time to complete the lesson before work and before getting my kids to school, then I would become a swimmer. My ability to master this new skill depended on my putting in regular effort with a coach to guide me.

When Coach Deichert first watched me, my swimming fears were immediately evident to him. Even better, it was so easy for him to end them. He obliterated my fears by having me use a combination of a nose-clip, to prevent water from getting in my nose, and earplugs, to keep the cold water out of my ear canals. Water invading me through my nose and ears was a habitual fear I had held onto since that surgery at age fifteen. The significant lessons here are (1) I didn't let a long-held fear deter me from pursuing a big goal, and (2) with the help of an expert, in this case a coach, I was able to quickly overcome a long-held fear.

The swimming portion of my triathlon was to be in a salty river. Therefore, I had to also train to develop swimming skills in open water, where there were no black lines on the floor to keep me swimming in a straight line. I had to learn to wear a wetsuit for safety, as it kept me buoyant in deep water. I would meet my friend, Joy Kelleher, at Lake Lanier to learn the very particular art of open-water swimming. The first two times just the feeling of that slick, tight, rubbery bodysuit, going from my ankles to my chin, intimidated me. I'm claustrophobic anyway, so I do not like feeling confined. Then add in the constriction of the neoprene across the chest, and it seemed I knew what emphysema must feel like. I would have to stop every quarter mile around the island to just slow my breathing and get rid of the wheezing.

Joy would be ahead in the lake, and stop and wait for me. Once I reached her, she assured me that my discomfort with the bodysuit was normal. "This is why we are meeting, to get you acclimated to the feeling. Keep coming, it gets better," she promised. And she was right.

By the third time, I was no longer claustrophobic, the wheezing was gone, and my arms had become accustomed to completing a mile through the resistance and pulling of the neoprene cloak. Notice here how again, with the help of an expert combined with regular practice, I managed to overcome some extreme discomfort and propel myself forward on the path to achieving a big goal.

Running—This was the only sport I was familiar with, but I learned a crucial lesson from it. I found out I suffered from "shiny object syndrome," a condition where I would lose my focus easily. It was in my running practice that I learned I suffered from this and that it was happening in all three disciplines.

This is how shiny object syndrome played out for me in my training. I'd get lost in the sunrise and boats while swimming in the lake, the other swimmers at the pool, and the multitude of pedestrians and dogs on my running route. The sensory overload while biking was at times too much to handle. I remember seeing birds flying, marveling at the architecture of dilapidated barns, and being intoxicated by the smells of cookouts and horse farms.

The consequences of shiny object syndrome— I'd bike, swim, and run more and more slowly as the distractions poured into my vision and in my nostrils. Andy Lowe cracked the whip once he saw the negative effects of shiny object syndrome on my training.

Andy demanded I bike the same route for each workout and run the same route for each run. He told me to keep my head down, focus, and crank out the workouts. He saw how much potential I had as an athlete, but that I was not yet tapping into it. He said he wanted me to almost be bored on my routes because of the repetition of it week after week. He wanted me to see nothing but faster times on my watch, higher heart rates, and more sweat on my face. I complied with his recommendations and got more serious and dedicated.

So again, my pursuit of my BIG DREAM didn't just entail devising a plan and doing it. I also depended on others for motivation, expertise, and help with both the long-held fears and unanticipated issues that surfaced.

In general I organized my week like this: (days 1 and 2) bike heavy two days; (day 3) use an off day to rest the legs; (day 4) bike fast a day; (days 5 and 6) run heavy for two days, which trashes the legs; (day 7) use the swim to rest the legs. Repeat.

Below, I'm going to share some of the specifics, just so you can get inspired about how I devised a schedule to work with my emotional, physical, and mental needs in order to make progress toward my goal. Remember too that all these times and distances are for the half Iron-distance triathlon training. Everything increased when training for the full Ironman.

Sunday—Long Bike

- This ride would be anywhere from one to four hours of cycling, or fifteen to fifty-six miles of cycling, building incrementally each week by fifteen minutes until the maximum time or distance was reached.

- The goal here was steady, slower-paced riding, designed to achieve one thing: conditioning the body to be able to stay in a biking position for the prescribed duration of the race.

Monday—Intermediate Bike

- This ride tended to be about one hour in length, at a moderately steady pace.

- The goal was to spin the lactic acid out of the legs that had accumulated from the long ride the day before.

- On working weeks, I would typically do this after work at home on my trainer in the evening, while watching mindless TV shows, like *The Middle* and *Family Feud*, with my kids.

- On off weeks, I'd bike at the sunniest time of day. I would bike circuits of a fifteen-mile loop.

Tuesday—Rest or Additional Swim

- Because I had so much to learn at the beginning, I met Coach Diechert at the pool for more lessons on my rest day. However, as time went on, I would take this day off.

Wednesday—Tempo Bike

- This ride was forty-five minutes in length, as fast as I could go.

- I always did this at home on my trainer, first thing in the morning, from 5:30 am until 6:15 am. I used trainer ride videos for motivation and extra challenge.

- By starting early, I could shower, get my kids to school by 8:15 am, and make it to work by 9 am.

Thursday—Tempo Run and Swim Drills

- This revolved around the availability of Coach Deichert.

- I aimed to be in the pool ready to swim by 5:30 am. Then I'd swim an hour.

- Coach Deichert called the shots here: a warm-up with snorkel, kicking drills, sprinting drills, etc.

- Then I'd quickly shower off the chlorine, drive home, change into running gear, and run four miles.

- The goal for the tempo run was to start with a warm-up mile and with each mile, run faster to shave off fifteen to thirty seconds, ending in my fastest possible mile. Andy said the purpose was to teach my body (and brain) that I can go faster with time. He explained that most people start out fast in runs (and in their lives) and go slower and slower, expecting less and less as time goes on. He urged me, "You have to show yourself that does not have to be the case."

Friday—Long Run

- The goal was a slow and steady pace, whatever pace I could manage to maintain for the duration of the entire distance. For me, that was a consistent eleven minutes per mile.

- I ran up and down Riverside Drive, near my house, and down historic Green Street and through a university campus.
- Keeping my house in the center of the route design, I could use my mailbox as an aid station, but I tried to strap every supply needed into my fuel belt.

Saturday—Long Swim

- I did this swim at the local pool or the lake.
- The goal of this workout was to swim the full distance of 1.2 miles.

Dreamer & Doer—Both

In addition to identifying your big dream and devising a plan for pursuing it on a daily basis, the crucial element to achieving that dream lies in committing to the plan you've devised. In following through with your plan, chipping away at it day by day—no matter how you feel, no matter the weather, no matter your other responsibilities—that's where push comes to pull. That's where the rubber meets the road. That's what separates the dreamers from the doers.

While I was working as a full-time doctor with children at home, each with their own practices to attend, a house to run, and a marriage to actively participate in, I also had to train six days a week in order to pursue my dream.

I remember times when my day of work would be stressful, but I had to wake up early the next day and train anyway. I couldn't allow minor illnesses, like an upset stomach or mild sinus problems, to stop me from meeting the day's goals. Even when I was on vacation, I'd have to swim and bike and run. What I'm trying to say is that you cannot let "life" get in the way of your dream.

So just as I'd been teaching and preaching to Wyatt and Jessica that they must practice, practice, and practice some more for their baseball and music-related dreams to come true, I had to do the same. And just watching my kids chip away at their own sports and schoolwork ended up giving me a tremendous amount of motivation. They gave me real-life, living and breathing examples to follow. They exemplified just what commitment had to look like for me to achieve my goal.

In order to follow through with my commitment to my practice schedule as well as my responsibilities as a mother, wife, and doctor, everything I did that was outside of the necessary had to be done quickly and efficiently. I started applying makeup at red lights. Laundry was done while listening to podcasts that helped me perform better. Online billing from the hospital was done at the dinner table. My husband, Steve, did so much to help. The kids were diligent about maintaining the household chores: putting away the laundry, trash, and recycling, and unloading the dishwasher. Other moms and dads pitched in to bring the kids home from school, practices, and games if my bike rides were running late, or if I'd gotten caught in traffic and Steve was stuck at work. Again, I depended on my family, colleagues, and friends to make it all work. They were essential to my success.

This commitment to do the necessary work is what separates the dreamers from the doers. It is really easy to say you're going to do something, lay down money, and do the necessary work a couple of times, or maybe even twenty times. But then most people give up. They lose sight, and they don't stay on the plan.

But when you're supposed to bike and it starts raining and you do the scheduled workout anyway, there's an unshakeable certainty that your dreams will come to fruition. Is it cold? And you are supposed to swim? You do it anyway. You start on a 2.5-hour run, and a storm comes. There's wind and some mild lightening. You continue anyway.

If you let the small obstacles—a change in the weather, a postponement of your workout by a couple of hours, or getting bailed on by your intended work-out companion—get you off your schedule, you are done. You won't do the work needed to finish the goal. You need a fierce, die-hard commitment.

Trust the Plan

And you have to trust the plan. Little bits of consistent effort will result in your achieving the big goal if done persistently over time.

I remember begging Andy to let me bundle two or three days' worth of workouts into one day, so I could have more than one day off a week. He refused. He urged, "Stick to the plan." In the end, I had to learn the hard way. For example, once I strayed from my intended plan and did my tempo run late at night. My next day's long run was scheduled to begin at 4:30 am the next morning, but I couldn't do it. My body demanded sixteen to twenty-four hours of recovery in between workouts. Doing too much too closely together would lead to injury. So I learned I had to stick to the original, set-in-stone plan.

I vividly recall once on the Fourth of July, I couldn't start my bike ride until after work, and my family was invited to a poolside cookout with a boat ride to see fireworks on the lake. I had to go bike in between work and the party, and be late to the party. When I was cycling, the smell of all the cookouts in the air fueled my fire to just persist, get it done, and then reward myself with the party. So I did it. But I think most people would have skipped that day's workout. I couldn't. That's an example of fierce commitment.

Staying On Track

I'm going to share the five essential elements that must be in place to stay on track to the plan you devise for achieving your long-term goal.

1. **Be organized**. I'm a visual learner. I meticulously and relentlessly sketched out on paper the entire seven months of workouts needed to make it to the start line of my half Iron-distance triathlon. I color-coded everything. Swim workouts were recorded in blue ink, the color of pool water; bike workouts in black, the color of my bike frame; and running workouts in red, the color of my face after running.

   I had two of these sketches. I placed one on the bathroom mirror, so it was the first thing I saw each day and the last thing I saw as each day came to a close. When I successfully completed the workout for the day, I circled it. My goal was to get as many circles for the week as I could. I then taped the second one on my refrigerator in my kitchen, so it was the last thing I would look at before I left for the day.

   I knew exactly when each workout would fit into my day and would prepare all work-out fluids and supplements ahead of time. I would write lists of what I needed to pack in my fuel belt, never forgetting things like ibuprofen, lip balm, and gum. I had a system of keeping all my gear for the three sports separate and accessible when needed. If my bike ride was going to last over three hours, I went ahead and packed my cooler the night before. I knew exactly how much water, bars, and gels I would need, so I either taped the gels to my bike, or I would break the bars into plastic bags.

For an extra measure, on day one of my workweek, I would quickly sketch out at the bottom of my patient list, that season's sports practices and music lessons, work meetings, and workouts of the week, so I had the desired outcome for the week ahead, right in front of me. And if three sets of my schedule failed to keep me on track, I even taped another on the dashboard in my car. Nothing was left to memory. It was in streaming color, in front of me, at all times.

2. **Get support from your family and colleagues. Don't try it alone.** None of my well-intentioned plans would have been (or would be) possible without the help of my husband. I informed him well in advance of what the week ahead would hold, when I would need him, how, and exactly where. It took a while for us, but eventually we became an unshakeable team.

I scheduled every last workout to have the least detrimental impact on my kids. Motherhood is my single most important job, and I did anything I could to tweak each day's work-out timing, so I could still be present in my kids' lives as much as possible. You have to have perspective, however. If over your kids' entire lives, you miss a game or two, as long as you do your best before and after your big dream acquisition phase, it will truly be okay. As parents, we are very accustomed to adjusting our schedules around all of our kids' events, and it is wise to teach them early on that your plans are important, too.

You have to be your own best advocate, take the initiative, and be specific with your loved ones. Tell your family what your limitations will be as you reach closer and closer to your goal. Remember, it's only for a season, not the rest of your life.

Secondly, at work I informed my colleagues of any backup I would need well in advance. On my workweeks, when it came time for the weekly long swim, I asked a colleague to cover my pager for the hour and a half. Again, it took some time to perfect. But as a working mom, most of us are accustomed to this constant juggle of doing the best we can at maintaining the self-work-kids triad anyway.

Again, it may sound laborious, but the bottom-line is this—where there was a will, I found twenty ways. Dreamers find excuses as to why everything gets in the way of obtaining their goals. Doers make it happen regardless. I saw every obstacle as a lesson in creative problem-solving. I am forever indebted to my colleagues and my husband for partnering with me to allow me to see my dream come true.

3. **Commit** to pursuing this dream, both for your own sake and as a model to your children. My philosophy is and will always be—if you say you're going to do something, do it. Make good on your word. I learned this from watching my parents every day growing up. If you say you're going to be somewhere, be there. I never wanted my kids to have to say, "Yeah, my mom, she said she was going to do an Ironman. I saw her swim and bike and run a couple of times. Then I don't know what happened. I actually don't even know when the race was supposed to be. But she never did it." Daggers! That would crush my spirit like a dagger to my soul! And I think that would crush my kids' spirits, too.

Wyatt would proudly proclaim to anyone who asked, "My mom? Yes! She is on track. Yeah, she is in the 'build phase' now. She's been at it for six months, I think. This Sunday she's missing one of my tournaments because she has a race simulation—where she bikes and runs for ten hours. Crazy, huh? Her race is in October. And she will become a winner on that day!"

4. **Allow for proper recovery.** I largely attribute my staying on track to my ability to properly recover after each workout. To me, recovery consists of three crucial elements: nutrition, supplements, and sleep. It is imperative to me that I eat at least five colors of fruits and vegetables each day. I limited my intake of refined carbohydrates and deep-fried foods, and never drank a sip of alcohol during my training.

Even still, a good diet can only get you so far. Even your best days can lead to some nutritional gaps. Each day I included four key supplements: omega-3 fatty acids, a probiotic to keep my innate gut immunity high, a multivitamin, and a calcium-vitamin D combination. Use whatever you want, but I only trust my body to AdvoCare products.

I also hired local nutrition coach, Betsy Pake, for further support. She placed me on a regimen of a certain ratio of carbs to proteins to fats. My endurance improved, and my recovery was more solid. As the cumulative effect of two years of training wore on my body, my diet, supplements, and sleep became pivotal to my success. Added together, Betsy's suggestions and the supplements were a winning combination for me. I have one word: game-changing.

Sleep was and will always be a priority in my life. Sleep is the only time the body has to do all of its repair work. I slept like I was getting paid! If you have to sleep in another room on the nights before a particularly early-morning task to achieve your goals, then do it. Either get your family on board to protect your sleep space, use an eye mask and earplug combination, or go to another room. But get your sleep. Nothing works well if you're sleep-deprived. I would recommend reading Shawn Stevenson's book *Sleep Smarter* to learn how to maximize the benefits of this crucial part of your day.

5. **Find an accountability partner.** It tremendously helps to share your dream and plan with someone else. That person serves as an accountability partner. Find other like-minded people to keep you true to your schedule and keep you motivated when you want to give up.

Even with excellent organization, support from family, friends, and colleagues, proper recovery and nutrition, and a steadfast commitment, there still will come times when you just don't want to do it. But you have to. That's what separates the women from the girls, as the saying goes. And you'll go through dark times that no one else will quite understand except for someone going through it too. I had a large support group of Ironman friends in and around town, and then I had my training partner.

Lisa Morris, friend and owner of Echo Wellness Center, was my accountability partner. She was training for her own Half Ironman a month before mine. The timing of our competitions was close enough together that we could help one another to keep on track. Although we couldn't do the same triathlon due to work conflicts, we either did the workouts together or texted our data to each other once we completed the task of the day.

It was crucial to me to have her there to celebrate things that may seem irrelevant to others, but were huge to us. We cried together, hated the plan together, failed together, and stuck to our plan together. We were there for each other through every drop of the blood, the sweat, and the tears. She was priceless in my journey.

In the next chapter, I'll share with you how it all panned out. You'll see the results of my big plan to achieve my half Iron-distance triathlon.

4

Milestone One: Putting It to the Test

Half Iron-Distance Triathlon, Beach to Battleship

After pursuing my plan over seven months with daily consistency and commitment, I was prepared to complete a half Iron-distance triathlon, a major milestone necessary on the road to my big dream of doing a full Ironman.

Because I had completed the prescribed daily workouts, all I had left was to do it. "Go be awesome," my coach instructed me. So awesome, I was. This is how it went down!

Swimming

The start time approached on the day of the race. I carefully secured my earplugs into place and tucked my hair into the bright yellow swim cap that signified I was in the wave that consisted of women over forty-five years old. I was in the last wave to start, at 9:02 am.

Group by group, we were instructed to enter the water and warm up. I stepped in and quickly got acclimated to the cold, salty water.

I waited for the bullhorn and started swimming. My swim lessons helped me easily get into a rhythm and do my bilateral breathing, accompanied by lifting my head every fifth stroke to spot the big, puffy orange and yellow buoys along the way.

Cycling

After the swim, came the bike. It was a fantastic fifty-six miles of the flattest, safest roads ever. It was the most well-marked route I ever dreamed possible. Learning to shift gears to bike hills and stay safe with other bikers, cars, and intersections had been very challenging for me. I had gotten lost; I had fallen off the bike; I had been left behind—everything imaginable. But through all of that, I'd prepared myself so well.

My nutrition and hydration on the bike were perfect. Through months of trial and error and hundreds of miles of testing, I had my nutritional needs down to a science. I ate solid food, drank a certain amount of sips of an electrolyte solution, and consumed gels at precise time intervals. I had to keep my energy up and my focus high. I followed my coach's recommendations to the letter. I knew the exact proportions of liquids to solids, carbs to proteins, and caffeine that I needed to fuel my body to endure the 70.3-mile distance. I was so thankful for my careful planning and my commitment to following through with it because that's how I was able to learn what my body required to manage this grueling race.

I could see by the pace on my watch that I was biking much faster than I ever had been able to manage in my training. My usual speed was fifteen miles per hour on long rides, and I was pulling sixteen miles per hour effortlessly. It wasn't easy though; the fingers on my right hand were numb, and it was impossible to get them to wake up.

I didn't need to stop at any of the aid stations. I had calculated, measured, and taped all of my own supplies with accuracy. It was my race; me versus 70.3 miles; that was it.

I finished the bike about thirty minutes ahead of schedule. This was an exceptionally proud moment for me: in the midst of all the cheering fans, metal grates, and volunteers in purple shirts, I flawlessly dismounted my bike. This is what I did: I very carefully unclipped my left foot and let it dangle. I stood up on the other pedal, braking slowly. Next I put my left foot down on the ground, but in a wide stance to increase my stability. Then I unclipped my right foot and swung my right leg over the bike's seat to dismount. My friend Melanie had spent hours teaching me this process, step by step. Because of her teaching and my commitment to learning and repeated practice of this dismount, I am proud to say that I scored!

Running—My Fight with Failure

When I changed into running shoes and began the 13.1-mile run, I was unexpectedly met with waves of intense and severe abdominal cramping. Grabbing my sides, I tried to muscle through, but the pain stopped me dead in my tracks.

I walked to aid station number one and described my symptoms, something no doctor ever likes to do. Doctors should be able to diagnose themselves; it's what we do for a living. As I was limping along, I started crying, wondering, "How on earth will I finish twelve more miles feeling like this?"

It was debilitating. I slowly jogged right into the medical area and asked for a bathroom, hoping that would help because maybe I just needed a break. I cooled off, pouring cold water all over my face.

When you're on the bike, the wind is hitting your face so hard that it can be difficult to tell how hot you really are becoming. I wondered if perhaps I'd overheated and hadn't noticed it until then. Or maybe it was the fact that I had eaten an enormous celebratory meal too late the night before the race. I had consumed coconut cake and many Vietnamese and Thai dishes that were not my norm.

So I had a serious talk with my reflection in the mirror, "You can do this. Just go out there and walk the whole thing if you have to."

But I'd trained so adequately for the run, and I wanted to run it. I started back but never regained my strength. Once I gave myself permission to start walking, I was walking intermittently throughout the whole half marathon.

I remembered the crucial part of the nutrition on the run: to consume my own gels, every three miles. I did this all through my training. Even still, I hit my all-time low at mile seven. It was 3:28 pm. I was at the 6.5-hour mark.

I couldn't bring music, and that was the only way I'd ever gotten through my long rides and runs. So I had nothing to distract me from the people. I had nothing to distract me from the pain. My slow pace made me feel like an absolute failure. If I had my phone with my familiar tunes, I could listen to "Total Praise" that had always told me when I was at my lowest,

> Lord, I will lift my eyes to the hills. Knowing my help is coming from You. Your peace You give me in time of the storm. You are the source of my strength. You are the strength of my life. I lift my hands in total praise to You.

I sang it to myself.

Eyes on the Prize

It all was a game of mental toughness at this point. I knew I was not going to give up and quit. I had no other choice than to finish this race. It was not turning out the way I'd expected, planned, or anticipated. Does anything? About a mile from the finish, my friend Denise ran back to find me and miraculously helped me find the ability to run again.

It took me a an exhausting seven hours and forty-one minutes to complete, but my first triathlon was in the books! I was officially a half Iron-distance woman warrior!

Half Iron-Distance Triathlon Lessons

Some lessons I learned that day were that commitment and consistency get you where you need to go. It had nothing to do with either skill or talent, as I had neither coming into this event. The greatest goals were accomplished by completing one tiny step at a time.

I learned I must believe in myself and my abilities, and only fill my mind space with positive thoughts and people. Limit or avoid negativity or doubt that will present itself in many ways. If you've followed your training schedule, the victory is yours before you even approach the starting line.

A constant and conscious wallpapering of your mind becomes imperative. Leadership books and motivational, educational podcasts helped to support my endeavors. If you encounter negative people who sneer at you, belittle your dreams, or call you crazy, please do yourself a favor and run, don't walk, the other way. Once you've signed up and committed to a dream, it is up to you to make it happen. And there's no space for the critics.

It's just like "The Man in the Arena" speech described, as spoken by Theodore Roosevelt in 1910:

> It is not the critic who counts; not the man who points out how the strong man stumbles, or where the doer of deeds could have done them better. The credit belongs to the man who is actually in the arena, whose face is marred by dust and sweat and blood; who strives valiantly; who errs, who comes short again and again, because there is no effort without error and short-coming; but who does actually strive to do the deeds; who knows great enthusiasms, the great devotions; who spends himself in a worthy cause; who at the best knows in the end the triumph of high achievement, and who at the worst, if he fails, at least fails while daring greatly, so that his place shall never be with those cold and timid souls who neither know victory nor defeat.

I knew in my heart that it was acceptable that the half Iron-distance triathlon didn't turn out exactly how I'd envisioned, but that I had done it anyway. And I did it while daring greatly. That was the longest endurance event I had ever accomplished. It was wonderful that I even dared to try. I also learned to "roll with the punches," and if things don't go as planned, to just dig deep and do what I can do. But the point is—do it.

When you've blown through your physical reserves, only your mental toughness remains. You have to be psychologically up to the challenge or you will fall off task. You learn a great deal about yourself at these times.

Points to Ponder

For me the half Iron-distance triathlon was a great way to benchmark my mind and body in my pursuit of the bigger dream, the Ironman. It's imperative to have meaningful, powerful benchmarks along the way as you pursue your bigger dream. Celebrate and cherish those.

The Half Iron-distance triathlon was now in my rearview mirror. The truths I discovered would be crucial to master the training for the full Ironman. In the next chapter, I share how, despite all the knowledge and training, I suffered a devastating blow at the full Ironman.

5

Race Day

Thirteen More Months to Prepare

The half Iron-distance triathlon served as a stepping-stone to the ultimate goal of accomplishing the full Ironman thirteen months later. The date of the race quickly approached.

A full Ironman is much more rigorous than the Half. So I vowed not to miss any workouts—rain or shine, cold or hot, early or late, with a companion or alone. I swam, biked, and ran just as the schedule dictated.

I had two years of training behind me, countless hours of perfecting my nutrition, conditioning my neck and back muscles, and getting a critical mass of mental toughness ingrained into my psyche.

Race Day

I was well-prepared and ready to knock it out of the park! A fully sanctioned Ironman-branded event brought with it a higher level of professionalism and rigor than the Half. Strict rules governed the thousands of athletes present. The sheer sight of hundreds of these lean, muscular bodies everywhere I turned, speaking all languages of the world, made my heart skip a beat.

I was calm, healthy, well-rested, and had no stress to speak of. I had Lisa, my mom, my sister, and my nutrition coach, Betsy, with me. And we were eating just as the suggested diet dictated, keeping away from fried-foods, refined sugar, and alcohol—a mistake I had naively made the night before the half Iron-distance triathlon.

On race day, the temperature in Florida where the race was taking place was unseasonably warm. Because of this, wearing a wetsuit incurred a ten-minute penalty. They'd explained it in the athlete's meeting the day before. There also were many other crucially important tidbits of information that I tried to cement into my memory. In the midst of all the rules, regulations, people, equipment, and transition bags to keep up with, I later learned I missed some rules.

Andy flew in from California to help us and to celebrate our crossing of the finish line together. I had a slew of emotions and concerns that I'd never before experienced. It was easier for me to take care of twenty critically ill patients in the ICU than to remember everything I had to remember for this Ironman competition.

Swimming

The ocean on race day morning was very choppy. As the race began, I carefully took what I felt was "my place" on the shore—at the very back of the line, at the back of a very long line of 3,300 athletes. Despite the penalty, I chose to have the extra safety and buoyancy of a wetsuit because I had never trained without one. Other athletes who were comfortable swimming proceeded without the wetsuit.

I gazed out at the horizon, watching six- to eight-foot oceanic swells greeting me. It was not a pleasant sight. I started to get nervous, but I was trying my very best to remain calm.

The swim was two laps of a 1.2-mile course. I joyfully remarked to Lisa, "This is going to be easy. Let's just pretend it's another day at our lake." I had successfully completed 2.4-mile swims at Lake Lanier week after week. That distance predictably took me one hour and fifty minutes to swim. Those had been long swims, cold swims, boring swims, and very lonely mornings and evenings.

Then the unthinkable happened: not more than two hundred yards into the swim, I was adjusting my nose-clip, and it BROKE IN HALF. My crutch was gone! I became horrified. I had never swum a single yard without my nose-clip. Now there were four thousand yards ahead of me to finish.

I frantically reached out to the nearby volunteers in their kayaks, screaming, "Does anyone have an extra nose-clip?" Of course, they didn't. I had to teach myself right then and there how to swim without a nose-clip. Hot, salty water started pouring into my nose and down my throat constantly. I was disappointed at my lack of skill for breathing properly without the clip.

The current was strong. The undertow was even stronger. The taste of ocean water and chocolate meal replacement shake kept coming up into my mouth. "Keep swimming, Cindy." Andy had told me, no matter what happens, on any leg of the triathlon, to just keep moving forward. I focused on relentless forward progression towards my goal.

At the halfway point, my Garmin watch read, "sixty-five minutes." The swim had never taken me that long. I had to hurry up and finish the second half. Cut off was two hours and twenty minutes. As I hurried to finish lap number two, I was a little concerned when some volunteers out at the buoys called to me, "Keep on swimming, girl, we want to see you get on the bike!" Time was obviously running out. I didn't check my watch, but just kept swimming. By now, I had gotten accustomed to exhaling through my nose to somewhat stop the water from making me feel like I was drowning.

One by one, I witnessed fellow athletes giving up, calling to the Sea-Doo drivers and being motored to the shore. I was now sharing ocean space with fewer and fewer swimmers. I was side by side with some of the handicapped athletes who were being carried by kayaks that attached to them.

I finally heard people cheering! I saw the shore! I welcomed the exit! I had just made it through the most treacherous swim of my life. I made a quick mental note to never, under any circumstances, ever swim in an ocean again.

I don't know what shocked me more—the sight of 2 hours, 12 minutes on my watch, which meant that I was a mere 8 minutes from the cutoff time, which meant disqualification; or the distance I had just traversed—3.1 miles. I couldn't take the time to think about that. Clearly that must have been an error or the undertow had taken me that many feet off course. I swam 3.1 miles in swim strokes to complete the 2.4-mile course.

I saw a familiar face at the exit volunteers, my Ironman lawyer friend from home, Bryan Baumgardner. He commanded me to not focus on anything about the swim. I had to let that go. I had to get on the bike. Now!

Cycling

The bike course was wonderful, sunny, scenic, and the best part—dry! It was so exhilarating to know I was doing it! I was in the Ironman! Ten miles, twenty miles, then once I reached mile forty, I hit a desolate patch of the route. I saw no other bikers for a couple of miles.

Unfortunately, I hadn't memorized the route, so I started to worry I was lost. I don't believe anyone likes being lost. Being lost, all alone, on a bike, in eighty-five-degree blazing sun, in the middle of nowhere, is especially unsettling.

I thanked God when I finally encountered an Ironman sign and got to turn off this stranded highway. I stopped at the next aid station.

I needed no supplies, but I stopped anyway because there was one thing there I needed on a deep, soul level—other human beings! Aid stations were located every ten miles or so. I was six hours total into my journey, and my body was aching. I stopped at every one I saw.

I even stopped at "special needs" though I needed nothing. I was now at a familiar place in the route at mile seventy-five. I was on a long stretch of ten miles looking to turn around and head back to the finish line.

The Official. The Rule. The Tears

It was 3:15 pm when I saw ahead an official standing with a clipboard. Ten athletes were standing around, all off of their bikes. I was confused. I saw a sixty-year-old male athlete leaning over a van, bawling. I saw no accidents, no blood, no crashes. An official approached me and asked me to hand him the timing chip from my ankle. I asked why.

He explained I had to be at the mile-eighty marker by 3:05 pm. It was 3:15 pm. I had not made it there in time. By the looks of it, there was no way around this hard fast rule, and the guy was pulling off another biker as we stood. What a strange feeling in the middle of my fifteen-hour day. I was standing still when I had either been swimming or biking for eight straight hours. You don't stand in Ironman. You fight, you swim, bike, and run, and then you conquer.

Watching grown men cry is the saddest thing to me. Seeing this official with a clipboard methodically record our names and numbers made me cry.

I was carted in a van with other unfinished, disqualified athletes to the transitional area. I walked in my socked feet to gather my bike. Just having to hold my biking cleats and helmet, I felt like a failure. These items were supposed to be given to me at 10 pm after I had tasted victory! I was not supposed to be holding them at 4 pm while the sun was out. I think I was somewhat in shock.

Shame and Pride and Errors

I took the undeniable walk of shame to meet my family. Betsy ran towards me, yelling, "Girl, I am so proud of you!" How could she say this? She was proud of what? Pride was the furthest emotion from my mind.

She explained to me that she was proud of me for getting in the arena (the premise of the "Man in the Arena" speech). She was proud of me for daring greatly, for toeing the line. She had already posted on Facebook, "If you're not in the rink getting your ass kicked, I don't want to listen to any of your opinions!" Mom, Gina, Betsy, and a disappointed but proud Andy did their best to cheer me up. It wasn't happening. I had one thing on my mind: running with Lisa.

I quickly headed to my run bag, containing my running shoes, to find her. I was greeted by yet another shocker: an official informing me I couldn't get to my run bag until the last biker finished the course.

I am not the type to challenge authority, but I do like to make sense of the rules I follow. He explained this ensured the safety of the bikers. I move on to plan B. I'll just go find her on socked feet and run with her. Again, I was unfortunately quickly versed in the strict rules of Ironman. I couldn't re-enter the racecourse as a DNF—*did not finish*—recipient. Period.

If I ran alongside Lisa, I would risk the chance of disqualifying her. That would be terrible if neither of us finished because of me. Andy suggested I go up to Lisa's condo and scrub off all identifying marks of me as an athlete. I did this and put his volunteer shirt on. I could then safely and legally enter the course, undercover as a volunteer.

I ran to find Lisa, and she was just finishing up her first half of the marathon. We embraced. I may have cried a little. She told me how sorry she was.

She was having some foot issues. I wished I could have foot issues. I was mad and jealous, but I quickly stuffed that down and helped her. We dug through her special needs bag to find Vaseline, Band-Aids, and fresh socks. I helped her get her feet dry. She looked good and was doing great!

I ran a mile with her in my socked feet but couldn't run any more. The concrete was hard, and burrs were getting stuck in my socks. I said my goodbyes, telling her to run strong for me and that she was doing awesome!

Sadness and frustration consumed me. I couldn't stand seeing the masses of athletes because it was making me feel more aware of my own failure with each passing runner. I was hungry too and felt like I was in the middle of the worst waste of an opportunity. Utter humiliation pervaded my brain.

Andy was quick to sum up what had happened— I'd made a clerical error. I missed the fact that there was a cutoff time in the middle of the bike course. I also had lost track of time on the bike and had gotten too far behind to complete on time. It wasn't the big waves in the ocean, the breaking of the nose-clip, lack of any skill, or inadequate training. I just wasn't aware of the cutoff times on the bike course. I had failed to calculate the hourly distance goals I needed to finish on time.

Right at that moment, I needed food, but I couldn't leave until Lisa crossed the finish line.

My mom, sister, Betsy, Andy, and I headed to Mellow Mushroom. It was far enough away that I couldn't hear all the cheers of the folks crossing the finish line.

I had my emotions under control and didn't feel like seeing anybody but this group of four safe people. These people had come to witness me accomplish the impossible dream, and I hated that I had let them down. I felt like they had come here for nothing.

I hoped they had had a good time without me. I had been no company to speak of, just a self-consumed athlete, getting the prescribed workouts in and demanding certain foods. Having to get off my feet and rest was part of my taper, so I wasn't even able to walk on the beach with my family.

After dinner and some moments of reflection, I went to the bleachers by the finish line to wait for Lisa. It was difficult to watch the athletes crossing the finish line. I knew then how it felt to want something so badly, to not be able to obtain it, and to watch someone else get it. Right then it was not about me. I shifted all of my attention to my training partner Lisa, and as I spotted her coming down the chute, I was utterly consumed with pride for her. That girl was as tough as nails.

During her Ironman journey, she battled the pressures of single motherhood, personal and business stresses, an illness, and now, debilitating blisters on her feet. They called her name, Andy placed the medal around her neck, and we were all so indescribably ecstatic.

So . . .

I've shared with you all the messy, difficult details of my big race day, the day I spent two years preparing for, so you can experience vicariously the fact that even after you relentlessly prepare to accomplish what may seem like an impossible dream, sometimes things don't go your way. And it is absolutely devastating on so many levels—publicly, personally, physically, and spiritually. And the devastation and feelings of failure don't just exist in that moment but beyond. They revisit you in your quiet moments alone and revisit you when acquaintances and friends back home ask you about it.

However, in spite of the depressing emotions, you can still tap into your logical, rational side to very carefully analyze the errors you made that caused the failure. Don't blame things that aren't meant to be blamed. From there you devise a plan to correct the error, meaning you try again. You learn from the experience and try again.

For me, whether I heard a hundred people a day on Facebook tell me, "You're not a failure!" "You're still a winner to me," and "I'm proud of you anyway," it didn't matter. The sting of my failure was still cutting deep. Those two single words "still" and "anyway" literally felt like razors on my skin. I slipped farther away from my core of strength.

Upon my arrival home, the minute I stepped in the door, Steve and my kids gave me the sweetest homemade poster and showered me with flowers, hugs, and dinner at my favorite restaurant. The poster read, "You're our Ironmom. We are so proud of you! Welcome home! We missed you sooooo very much!" That, too, was sweet, but not enough to lift me out of the depression that consumed me.

Andy quickly became one of the most powerful and effective weapons in my arsenal to stop the negative thoughts. He helped me to unleash the warrior inside that was always there. It's almost like I needed a non-relative to assure me I was not a failure. I had to hear it from a person with an objective point of view.

Anyone who thinks they can't afford a mindset coach should consider instead that they can't afford to *not* have one. Do not ever go it alone when you're trying to undo psychological trauma. Talk to a pastor, a counselor, a trusted friend, but don't ever try to get out of the depths of depression all-alone.

Once I could be more objective about the whole experience, I did realize my failure was not due to a lack of training or a missing skill. I lacked the knowledge of cutoff times, that's all. And that's why I didn't see my big dream come true that day. It was then up to me to choose to make this error into a helpful tool that I could put in my toolbox to aid me in my next go-around.

In the next chapter, I share with you two methods that helped me sort through these raw, debilitating emotions and move on to success.

6

Something Lost, Something Learned

Do you want your kids to give up if they hit one stumbling block? What did I tell Wyatt when he pitched a poor outing on the mound in baseball? I told him to focus on what he could do and to get out there and keep going!

So you just read my account of the most crushing failure of my life. In this chapter I will reveal some key skills I used that you too can use to help you put perspective on a failure. This helps you determine where and how to move forward.

When I returned home, reality began to set in. Being a leader in my community, I knew people were going to watch how I reacted to this failure. The pain that I felt was temporary, as acute and devastating as it was. But how I moved forward would have an everlasting effect on me, my family, and my community.

I had to have a redo. To me, it was as if I had studied for a test and failed it, and I saw another chance to pass the test. I was interviewed for a podcast shortly thereafter, and I morbidly explained how I was feeling—as if I had been pregnant for nine months but had a stillborn birth. Then God showed me one tiny thing I could have changed to correct it, to undo the pain, and He showed me a second chance at life. And just as I'd encourage anyone—as I'd already encouraged Wyatt—when you get a second chance, go for it.

List Making & Letting Go

Despite the certainty that I should attempt another Ironman, I could barely stand the thought of redoing the preparation. Fellow colleague and Ironman friend, Drew Abernathy, challenged me to take some time and compose lists of what I liked about the training and what I didn't like. He quickly noted that for him, training for an Ironman strengthened some relationships and severely strained others and that he would never do another.

Fellow world-athlete Ironman and lifeguard friend Mitch gave me another exercise: write down everything that went wrong that day and everything that went right that day. And then, most importantly, he demanded I not think about it anymore. He wanted me to give myself a break from it.

I searched deep in my soul for guidance, and two weeks later, I had my answer: it was never a question of *if* I was going to cross the finish line of an Ironman; the question was *which* Ironman finish line I was going to cross. I researched and found three choices. I could (1) repeat the same Ironman in Florida in a year, (2) go to Cozumel in two weeks, or (3) compete in a HITS brand of a full iron distance triathlon in Naples, Florida in two months. These were my choices.

I didn't want to repeat a whole year of training, and I could literally feel the fitness still present in my body. I didn't want to waste all the conditioning that was in my muscles right then. When you go through the general prep and build phases of training, you develop a remarkable amount of sheer cardiovascular fitness and stamina that is undeniable.

Cozumel Ironman was on Thanksgiving Day, and I just wanted to be home with my family then. So I chose Naples, two months away, and Coach Andy quickly sketched out the details of the training I would need to complete it. Then I got to it.

A Slight, But Important Difference

But I couldn't go public this time. I was too public with my first attempt. I hated having to rehash the details of my failure daily, sometimes several times a day, to people at church, people at work, people at my kids' school, and people at my son's baseball and basketball practices.

It made me too vulnerable. I was tired of crying, and those conversations inevitably would elicit tears. I didn't have time for that. My mindset needed to be strong, tough. So I couldn't be transparent this time.

I also couldn't keep beating myself up for the past mistakes that I'd made. I had to take the advice that I had learned, apply it, and do better this time. Failure helps you to learn and grow. This time, it was all about me. It wasn't about doing it for anybody else. I didn't need to see or hear or read that anyone else was proud of me.

In Romans 10, I have learned that you don't have to live your life always looking for acceptance. That work was done on the cross a long time ago. If you look for the outside world to validate you, that can lead to people-pleasing, affairs, addiction, obsession with food, and acceptance by other people. The only true value comes from God. And that comes for free.

I surmised that I had been too consumed by looking for feedback and approval from others. I shared too many details. I had even been the featured subject in a local magazine article. Lisa and I were on the front page of the sports section of the *Gainesville Times*. Everyone knew of the race, and now they all also knew of my failure.

In summary, I had to have a redo. The steps I took to help me decide what I needed to learn from my failure and where to focus my attention next were as follows.

First, I made a list of my likes and dislikes of training. I liked the science behind the progression of the three sports. I loved recording my paces and

seeing them improve. I loved how if you d(
exceptionally long race simulation, then your long
run for the week got to be shorter, and you got to
remove the intermediate ride from the week's agenda.
What I didn't like was doing the workouts by myself.
I hated biking on roads with traffic. Long bike rides
were my least favorite part of the whole schedule due
to danger, the extreme time involved, and boredom.

Second, I delineated what went right the day I
failed and what went wrong. I aced my nutrition, the
swim, and the first portion of the bike. What went
wrong was my lack of knowledge of the eighty-mile
cutoff time, and spending too much time at the aid
stations. Both of these errors I knew I could easily
remedy in my next go.

Third, I stopped thinking about it and gave myself
a break. During my break, I spent concentrated time
on swimming and lots of time with my family. I also
enjoyed taking a break from biking and running.

Finally, I decided I'd do another full Iron-distance
triathlon but be much more private about it.

The next chapter chronicles the amazing,
effortless success I experienced a short two months
after my initial, devastating failure. Yes, rebounds
are possible after a big, seemingly impossible failure.
And perhaps, the success from the rebound is even
sweeter because of that initial, huge fail . . .

7

Race Day, Take Two

Two Months of Advanced Prep

The oddest thing happened the minute I signed up for the race in Naples, Florida. It was as if the skies opened up and little angels in all shapes and forms were materializing in front of my eyes and coming out of the woodwork to support my dream.

My friend, Joy, who had helped me two years previously to learn the art of open-water swimming with a wetsuit sent me an instant message. She offered me her services to shave some time off my swim and build some strength to fight the undercurrent if I have to swim in similar conditions again.

A triathlete friend and local triathlon store owner, Ginny Crumley, gave me the most precious bracelet that has the engraved message, "She believed she could. So she did." Coincidentally, my father's girlfriend had given me a coffee mug with the exact same message on it two weeks earlier. The universe seemed to be affirming my steadfast commitment to my goal.

I did believe I could. And I was about to do it.

My friend Mitch who is also a lifeguard helped me to research the tide charts for the day of the full Iron-distance triathlon in Naples and educated me on swim conditions. Fellow Ironman friend Randy Allen found out the wind directionality on race day and foretold the sections of the bike route where I would gain time due to tailwinds and lose time because the wind would be in my face.

Joy met me at the local pool and had me perform drills like I had never done before. Timed drills, sighting drills, sprints, technique, and form. She even had me complete a portion of each day's swim with a contraption strapped to my waist that looked like a parachute. Its purpose was to collect water and give the resistance that waves in the ocean can give. It was awful—but very helpful.

There was one point when I thought Joy was surely trying to make me drown, and I told her that I didn't like her very much. She quickly assured me that she was not there to make me like her, but to get me across that finish line of the full Iron-distance triathlon.

Ginny helped me take Andy's plan that I had to follow and made it more doable as a mother during both Thanksgiving and Christmas holidays. Every week I had to run a half marathon, and it seemed like I always got caught in the rain or was running on an unseasonably cold day. One time I literally had to wear four layers of hats and neck gators just to protect my face from the bitter cold.

When I found myself complaining, my support staff of Ironman friends put all of it into perspective. Mitch said he always wanted his training days to be miserable so that he had those experiences if the weather turned bad on race day, "If everything is perfect during training, you'll be ill-prepared for race day conditions that might be less than ideal."

Race Day, Again

Despite a momentary breakdown at 6 am when I started sobbing in my mom's arms while doubting my ability to successfully accomplish the full Iron-distance triathlon before me, I found myself in a perfect situation. The ocean was calm, and the weather cool. As I donned my friend Melanie's wetsuit, I found myself enveloped with a sense of confidence.

Swimming

Following the advice of Joy and Andy, at 7 am when the bullhorn sounded, I placed myself in line right where I truly belonged, where strong swimmers go. I started in the middle of all the hundreds of swimmers. I did not hold back at the end of the line to somehow give myself a false sense of security. That would be old-Cindy behavior, and there was no room for that today.

The ocean honestly seemed as flat and quiet as Lake Lanier. I finished in an hour and forty-six minutes, almost twenty minutes faster than the previous Ironman. And I was able to get into my bike gear in a record seven minutes, thus shaving three minutes off my transition time!

Cycling

When I got on my bike, the air was filled with a decadent fog. I knew I would be biking from approximately 9 am until 5 pm, so the more overcast it was, the cooler and the easier it would be to bike for eight long hours.

I relentlessly followed the time and distance cutoffs that I had calculated for myself. I wrote them out and safely sealed the paper in a plastic bag. I did all my training bike rides with that paper taped on my aerobars. I also included in that bag a miniature map of the bike course.

I noticed early on the bike course that a policeman was following me. He was there to alert the policemen at each intersection that there was an athlete approaching and to stop all traffic in all directions to assure my safety. Well, I never knew the benefits that would come with being one of the slowest swimmers (which meant one of the tail-end bike riders)!

Having that policeman behind me made me feel literally like God was protecting me. I entertained thoughts of wondering if my mother had hired a personal private policeman for me because she knew how much I did not like biking on open roads. "No way she could have pulled that off," I told myself.

I honestly felt like things couldn't have gone more perfectly that day. Between the advantage the two previous triathlons had given me, idyllic weather, perfect ocean condition, and the policeman chaperone, I felt like I was almost cheating!

Once I had gotten through the first fifty miles of the course, I was out of the traffic-filled business district. That policeman left and never returned. Hour by hour I continued to make my distance goals and finally felt like victory was mine, as long as nothing unexpected happened . . .

My aunt and uncle, having joined my mom and Lisa, became a traveling cheering section. They saw me three times on the swim and five times on the bike. It was great having my friends and family there to support me. I knew it could be exhausting to be a spectator of the sport, and I was so thankful for their presence there.

My mom once told me as long as she could, that she would make sure to be at every competition I ever participated in. That's the kind of mom I am, too. What better place is there to be in this world than supporting your loved ones and giving them that boost they need to keep pushing when times get hard?

There were a few times when I did not know if I was going to be able to make it on the bike. I tried to stay so focused and not take any breaks so that I would make my time goals. My crotch was suffering the consequences of the subsequent pressure load. I knew that what I was feeling would heal in time. I just endured the pain and kept going.

Every time I really started struggling out there alone on those long highways with no other bikers around and no volunteers and cheering section, I would look up. There were always birds. They were always in groups of two.

My dear friend Melanie had called the night before my race and promised me that if I would just focus on what I was grateful for that day of the full Iron-distance triathlon, that God would help me in my journey. Her mother had recently died an unexpected and untimely death. Her mom's spirit had always shown up in Melanie's life as a bird. I couldn't help but think that those two birds were the spirit of Melanie's mom and my grandmother who had passed away two years previously. The birds could have also been Melanie's mom meeting up with the husband of my friend Wanda Adams who had just passed away less than four weeks before this race.

I would watch those birds, and no matter what pain I was feeling on that course, just their presence made me know that the precious souls of loved ones who had recently passed were out there with me. If they could trade places with me, they would. So I just kept going, steeped in the awareness of just how grateful I was to have the legs and the neck and the back and the arms to be able to endure this 112-mile bike ride. Thank you, Melanie!

I had forgotten sunscreen on some areas, and the sun really started coming out between the hours of two and four. I felt myself getting sunburned and hotter despite strong winds in every direction. There's no doubt about it, the full Iron-distance triathlon is tough. You realize what you're made of when you're doing these things. Your strength and mental fortitude become unshakeable.

Once I passed mile eighty on the route, I had completed more than I was allowed two months previously in Ironman Florida. I knew the worst was over. All I had to do was run a small marathon! This bad boy would be behind me. I biked to the finish line and was at least thirty minutes ahead of schedule!

That's all I needed to complete the full Iron-distance triathlon. Just as I had sketched it out, being a little faster on the swim, shaving a little time off in the transition, and diligently keeping to my fifteen-mile-an-hour pace on the bike, I now had plenty of cushion time to successfully complete the marathon no matter what. That was my strategy, and I was executing it perfectly!

Running

Doubt never entered my mind that I could finish the 26.2-mile run. I changed into my running clothes and began the marathon. This triathlon was much less strict than the Ironman-branded one in Panama City Beach. Lisa was allowed to run right next to me for as long as she wanted. She ran with me the first six miles.

This is what I had wanted to do with her at her Ironman, but I was prohibited. She talked me through the scorching body heat that I was feeling. She showed me how to bend my head forward and saturate my hair with ice water, not allowing the water to get on my feet as she had mistakenly done that had caused blisters in her race.

Once I cooled down, I was able to get into a rhythm of running. Lisa then got on my bike and biked alongside me the next six miles, and I really appreciated the company. At the halfway point, I refilled all my fuel bottles and visited with my mom for a couple of minutes.

I wasn't sure which way to re-enter the course, and I found it funny that some medical professionals started immediately tending to me because they thought I was disoriented. I quickly told them I was fine, and they could leave me alone.

A torrential downpour of rain came at mile twenty, right as I began the final six-mile lap. I thanked God right then and there for all the rainy, two-plus-hour training runs that I had endured. The most recent one was on Christmas Day. Rain couldn't stop me, nothing could.

This is what Ironmen are made of, right? We endure no matter what. I remember seeing "Don't quit" tattooed on Andy's wrist. It's true. It's what we do. All the remaining athletes started speaking words of encouragement more diligently to each other during that last hour. It was about 10 pm, and we were now in the fifteenth hour of constant exertion.

The raindrops were big and falling hard, making it hard to even see the path ahead. *Good job. Keep it up. You got this. Strong work*. We were doing it.

From time to time I had been feeling some intense cramping occurring in my intestines, and for a moment, my medical background got the best of me. I thought surely I could be suffering from lack of blood flow to my intestines. What if I had to get a portion of my colon removed after this was all said and done? I had heard stories of some ultra-endurance athletes experiencing bloody diarrhea and intestinal shutdown necessitating removal of the dead gut. I didn't want that to be me.

The porta-potties that were on the trail were at their maximum capacity by this hour of the evening with this many athletes having completed one of the toughest endurance events in their lives. I slowed myself down and walked for the majority of those last six miles just to make sure I didn't have to use the facilities and that I didn't have any accidents. I met a sweet couple from Canada who had done seven such competitions together, and we charged toward victory.

I knew Mom and Lisa must have been worried, sitting in that rental car, during this horrible storm. And part of me wanted to run as fast as I could just so we all could go home. But I also wanted to not have any accidents or soil the rental car. So I walked.

For the last quarter-mile, once the finish line was in sight, I picked up my pace and ran toward the officials. At 11:01 pm, Lisa grabbed the medal out of the man's hand and placed it around my neck. I was utterly elated and relieved all at the same time, and reality was hitting me just how strong I was. I had just swum, biked, and ran for sixteen hours, one minute, with no breaks! Victory sure is sweet and worth every bit of the pain and inconvenience that I lived through! You really develop iron into your soul during the process.

Bitter Humiliation to Sweet Victory

So after the bitter humiliation of an initial fail, I successfully retaliated—trained even smarter and made the errors from my disqualification into special learning tools to ensure my success in this second go-around. I dreamed big and twenty-six months later achieved that big dream.

As I say, if I can do it, you can too. You can follow the exact same steps I did to overcome any failures and eventually achieve the big dream you've set for yourself.

But achieving the victory on your "race day" is not where it ends. I want to share with you how to globalize your success. Using this simple God-given gift—of practicing each and every day, in spite of minor and major setbacks to achieve a big dream— you inspire others, perhaps thousands or millions of people. Now imagine that—planet Earth where people of all ages and backgrounds dream big and work consistently to achieve those dreams—and then support others in doing the same. Let's make that happen!

8

Beacon of Hope

In life, we all go through trials and tribulations. Each one hopefully makes us a better person. Think about this though—if we selfishly keep our lessons to ourselves, no one else benefits from them. It's almost as if the painful failure or mistake gets wasted if it only affects the one who failed. If we can look outside ourselves and share our experiences with others, our lowest points can inspire others in ways you never knew possible. Everyone can grow from what each of us may see as a mistake.

Julie's Example

Let's examine this in terms of the Ironman competitions. Through Ironman competitions, ordinary people can do something extraordinary. Look at Julie Moss in 1982. She exemplifies the spirit of Ironman. She was a college student working on her thesis in exercise physiology when she signed up for the 1982 Kona Ironman. She was poorly undertrained and severely dehydrated as she started the marathon portion of the race.

Somehow, though, she found herself in first place with a twenty-minute lead. She was the number one woman in the race. Unfortunately, four miles from the finish line, she collapsed from debilitating muscle cramps. Through fierce persistence and commitment to finish the race set before her, and despite multiple collapses on the trail, Julie Moss crawled her way over the last forty yards to the finish line.

It really didn't matter who won that day. Julie Moss, in second place, changed the sport forever and inspired millions. Learning of Julie's struggles and eventual race completion moves thousands, maybe even millions, of us to dig deeper, try harder, and attempt the seemingly impossible.

And there doesn't have to be anything that makes you not complete any goal that God puts in your heart or that you can dream of.

And Me

There is nothing extraordinary about me. I didn't know how to swim. And I was scared to death to get on a bike. I was simply a working mom. I did not come into this as a cyclist or a college swimmer or having been a runner all my life.

Where I was in my day-to-day life was a doctor with a husband and two children. I suffered from the same challenges everyone does, maybe even worse: perceived lack of time and no big pockets of space to add in huge time blocks for exercise. I wasn't working a nine-to-five job Monday through Friday, but I was under even more constraints because I worked seven days on and seven days off, and the days that I was working, I was on call for twenty-four hours a day. So I had to fight for my dream, literally and diligently.

In the twenty years after medical school, I had not accomplished anything amazing. Yes, I landed a great job. I had two awesome babies with an incredible man. We live in the most beautiful home in Gainesville and are members of a wonderful church. But I was not particularly athletic or active. Honestly, I did not have any outside hobbies and no personal interests to speak of. I was in the same boat that you are.

Lessons for All of Us

I learned a lot of lessons on the way to my full Iron-distance triathlon finish line. My journey instilled in my heart truths that I will never forget as long as I live.

Because I got that DNF, obviously, I needed to learn a few more lessons before I was able to cross the finish line of a full Iron-distance triathlon. Despite the perfect training plan set before me, the diligent commitment to and execution of that training plan, and the relentless carving out of time for the workouts day after day, I still did not cross the first finish line I encountered. I messed up the execution of the plan on race day!

In the world of triathlons, there are a certain number of people that decide to do a triathlon. Despite their self-limitations, they decide to shut up the naysayers and go after their goals. They choose to focus on what they can do, instead of what they cannot do. And little by little, day by day, inch by inch, mile after mile, freestyle stroke after freestyle stroke, putting pedal over pedal, and one foot in front of the other, a certain percentage of those who decide to sign up for a triathlon actually go through the process and train.

It's a strange thing to me, but then an even smaller percentage of those that train actually shows up to the race and attempts it. It takes a heck of a lot of courage to toe the line. To put your toes on that start line and hear that gun go off, so maybe that scares some people to death. But you'll never accomplish any goal by staying on your sofa! The only way to cross the finish line is to show up to the starting line.

Out of the small percentage of athletes that decide to do a triathlon, train for it, and show up for it, a certain portion of those complete the race. And that crossing of the finish line completes their story. Others, like me and twenty-six percent of the others in that first Ironman race that day, do not complete the race. They get disqualified or they have an injury and they get a DNF. The majority of the athletes' stories end right there.

Mine didn't though. I have found myself in a rare group of people, a very small group of stubborn, relentless chasers after a dream, which has given me a lifelong, compelling story to share. I had twenty seconds of courage, so I signed up for the second race. I crossed my finish line—just not the one I thought I would cross.

I changed one thing—I paid closer attention to the time and mapped out an hourly plan to keep me on track so that I could manifest and execute what I had successfully trained for. The realization of my goal will forever be wallpapered in my mind. Even thinking about it now jerks the tears right out of my eyes.

I felt huge that day, ten feet tall. I fought so hard for what I knew I was capable of. I became a local hero, of sorts. I feel like I could do anything now. I feel ironclad.

And I am convinced that if I can do it, everyone can. You can. We all can get whatever it is we want out of life.

The Ripple Effect

Moms come up to me at the middle school plays with tear-filled eyes to tell me I am their hero. Others tell me they watched my story unfold on Facebook and that they're so proud of me. "What persistence!" they all say. "I don't see how you did it."

A common theme I hear is that they were living vicariously through me, that they have an injury that prevents them from completing anything like this. Some of the men are envious because I've now done more than any of them have. And that gives my smile an extra layer of depth and a confidence that will forever be laced into my countenance.

I remember reading about and watching a video of a handicapped biker that was able to not only bike with one hand but could even change a tire using nothing but his hand and his mouth. He made me keep on going on race day when parts of my body literally felt like they were going to split wide open.

I drew on the strength and courage of the American soldier and war hero Louie Zamperini from the book and movie *Unbroken*. I remembered the scene where he got hit by all those hundreds of soldiers, and he woke up the next day and kept fighting for his life. I thought, "If he could survive getting hit by all those soldiers, who am I to let a small race disqualification hold me back from achieving my dream?"

A ship is beautiful when seen in a harbor, but it is not meant to sit in the harbor. We were not made for small; we were made for big and enormous things. Do not hide! Just as Matthew 19:26 says, God-sized dreams are "impossible without Him, but all things are possible with God!"

Our deepest fear is not that we are inadequate. Our deepest fear is that we are powerful beyond measure. It is our light, not our darkness that frightens us. We ask ourselves, "Who am I to be brilliant, gorgeous, talented, fabulous?"

Actually—who are you not to be? You are a child of God. Your playing small does not serve the world. There is nothing enlightened about shrinking so that other people won't feel insecure around you. We are all meant to shine, as children do.

We were born to make manifest the glory of God that is within us. It's not just in some of us; it's in everyone. And as we let our own light shine, we unconsciously give other people permission to do the same.

As we are liberated from our own fear, our presence automatically liberates others.

—Marianne Williamson

I wrote that in my own handwriting and posted it on my refrigerator a few years ago, and I continue to read it every day. I make sure all that enter my house read it, too.

So in summary, if you dream big, put yourself out there, and unfortunately, find yourself in the position where you have failed—don't worry. God will send people to lift you up, so you'll succeed on your next try. But you have to keep your eyes open and your ears tuned to those around you.

It's the same with other areas of life. As long as you listen to your heart, it is as if the universe opens up and sends you exactly what you need. God will make His plan work. He makes it all right. He protects us. And He will send us help.

God put us here to help and encourage each other. When the thought of another human being comes across your mind, reach out to that person. God puts in us this tremendous responsibility and gift to encourage each other.

An unspoken word is like a seed that is never put in the ground. That seed, once planted and sprouted, becomes words of praise, hugs, texts, prayers—those are like trees that have huge, outstretching branches. But you have to diligently, persistently, and carefully listen to those around you. They are all telling you their needs if you just get your face out of your cell phone, move your eyes from off the floor, and look up. Look in the eyeballs of people God puts in your path. They need you.

Be a living, breathing being of encouragement. It's one of the greatest jobs we are enlisted to do during our short time on Earth.

If and only if you start living an inspired, courageous life and if you start dreaming big, you'll set out a bright light and become a beacon of hope. That bright light will help others push past the small boxes that each of us lives in.

And don't hesitate to contact me at www. cindystarke.com to share your failures and successes! Let's kick the lid off our lives!

From Fear and Failure—To the Finish Line
Unleash Your Potential,
and Discover the Champion Within

By
Cindy Buckner Starke, MD, PhD
Wife, Mother, Doctor, Full Iron-Distance Triathlete

Reading Guide

Chapter 1—Fear's Roots

It helps to review the role of fear and failure in your own life. Identify the moments in your life from which you developed limiting beliefs. We all have them.

By identifying the moments from which your limiting beliefs stemmed, you can gain some voice and say over the moment and the limiting belief. You can turn the tables and take back control.

Chapter 2—From Let Down to Not Letting Up

Don't get so deeply entrenched into a daily grind that doesn't include pursuing bigger dreams and trying out new experiences. Keep a big dream, the one that may scare you to death, always in your mind. Remember what your dreams were as a kid.

Chapter 3—Devise a Plan & Commit

After spending some time dreaming, identify a goal that you're passionate about. Commit to meticulously learn the skills needed, no matter how long it takes.

Divide your big goal into incrementally smaller monthly, weekly, and then daily actionable goals. Be organized about reminding yourself what it will take to get where you're going.

Commit in your heart to pursuing the plan daily, no matter how inconvenient and uncomfortable it may feel weeks and weeks into the plan.

Get an accountability partner, the support of your family, and a small tribe of like-minded individuals to lean on.

Put it all into action. Eat well, take the key supplements I mentioned, and carve out the time to get good sleep to be at your peak performance.

Added together, they lead to the accomplishment of the big goal.

Chapter 4—Milestone One: Putting It to the Test

For me the half Iron-distance triathlon was a great way to benchmark my mind and body in my pursuit of the bigger dream, the Ironman. It's imperative to have meaningful, powerful benchmarks along the way as you pursue your bigger dream. Celebrate and cherish those.

When you've blown through your physical reserves, only your mental toughness remains. You have to be psychologically up to the challenge or you will fall off task. You learn a great deal about yourself at these times.

Chapter 5—Race Day

If you attempt your dream and dare greatly by jumping into the arena, but unfortunately fail, the world will not stop spinning. In spite of the depressing emotions, you can still tap into your logical, rational side to very carefully analyze the errors you made that caused the failure. Don't blame things that aren't meant to be blamed. And then devise a plan to correct the error, meaning you try again. You learn from the experience and try again.

Chapter 6—Something Lost, Something Learned

Think about how you can get yourself refocused and back in practice after suffering a big setback. How do you psyche yourself back up again and go for it another time?

Follow the four steps I outlined at the end of this chapter.

Chapter 7—Race Day, Take Two

I shared with you how I bounced back, stepped up my training, and dug even deeper into my spirit to replace a failed experience with one of success.

Use any parts of my story that resonate with you and imagine if you ever fail, how you can have your own bounce-back.

Write that new success story down, and spend time each day visualizing it. Making it real in your mind in combination with your daily practice will only ensure that you achieve it come your "race day"!

Chapter 8—Beacon of Hope

Take a moment and reflect—who in your life has been a beacon of hope? Think of both the famous, the historical, and also the local.

Now consider how you have been, are, or can be a beacon of hope to others. How can you provide more encouragement and support?

Are you pursuing your big dream yet, practicing what you preach and teach? I've shared my story with you in this book. I've given you all so many tips, systems, and steps. Now it's your turn to put it all in effect.

NOW IT'S YOUR TURN

Discover the EXACT 3-step blueprint
you need to become a bestselling author
in 3 months.

Self-Publishing School helped me, and
now I want them to help you with this

FREE VIDEO SERIES!

Even if you're busy, bad at writing, or
don't know where to start, you CAN write
a bestseller and build your best life.

With tools and experience across a variety
niches and professions, Self-Publishing
School is the only resource you need to
take your book to the finish line!

DON'T WAIT

Watch this FREE VIDEO SERIES now,
and Say "YES" to becoming a bestseller:
https://xe172.isrefer.com/go/curcust/
cmbucknerstarke

Urgent Plea!

Thank you for reading my book. I'm so very grateful for you.

I really appreciate all of your feedback, and I love hearing what you have to say.

If you enjoyed my story,

please leave a helpful REVIEW on Amazon.

Thank you so much!

Cindy

About the Author

Cindy Starke, an Atlanta native, is happy to call Gainesville, Georgia her home. She is married to Steve, and they have two beautiful children, Jessica and Wyatt. They have an aloof cat, Sammy, and a mischievous pit bull and Jack Russell Terrier mix, Ben.

Cindy got her BS in Genetics from the University of Georgia, her MD and PhD from Emory, and since 2007 is a shareholder physician at the Longstreet Clinic. She is actively involved at the Gainesville First United Methodist Church. She practices medicine at Chestatee Regional Hospital in Dahlonega at the foothills of the Appalachian Mountains.

When she's not running, biking, or swimming, you can most likely find her at Jessica's tennis or volleyball games, or watching Wyatt play baseball or basketball. Her favorite pastimes are listening to Jessica sing and play guitar, ukulele, banjo, and piano, travelling, spending time with her mom and sister, hiking, fishing with her brother, David, tent camping in the mountains, building fires, and baking homemade bread and cakes.

She enjoys helping others find their healthiest, most energetic version of themselves. Her dream is to be a beacon of hope to help others find health rather than succumb to the devastating illnesses so prevalent in America.

Please contact Cindy at http://cindystarke. com/contact to let her know how *From Fear and Failure—To the Finish Line* inspired you to pursue a big dream, get past a difficult failure, and live life to its utmost.